All The Things You Never Asked

All The Things You Never Asked

Poetry

by Nicholas Bonarski

Dedicated to Nicole
for inspiring the challenge...

Forward

This book started out as a conversation about the number of journals that I keep and the ungodly amount of notes that I have stored in my phone notes app at any given time. Throughout the day, especially at work, I'll record random thoughts, poems, and conversations with myself as a way to get closer to what I actually think and feel. It serves as a way to empty my mind, entertain myself, and sometimes digest the feelings that I have at the time I'm recording them.

Everything in this book at some point served as catharsis for me. I would write what I needed to, quickly separate from it, and forget it ever existed. A good practice for a private person with a penchant for writing. Lo and behold, everything was still there.

The more poetic phrases of this book are from failed writings or poems that I started and never returned to. Some poems in this text, I didn't feel a particular attachment to, and so left behind. In some instances, a passage of this book may be the record of a dream I had during the night. I've been an avid dream collector for years and frequently record them as practice for recalling details of them to increase my awareness in the dream state and also to add a few new images into my writing repertoire. Over the years, my dreams have become a lot more vivid thanks to this, and I'm happy that a few of them have a place here in the pages ahead.

The challenge was to take a sample of my notes to create a collection of writing with, to arrange them in a new and interesting way as an attempt to tell a story through them, placing them in whatever position they happened to fit best in. What I have is an intimate look into my own thinking over the last few years.

This sample was taken (mostly, but with a few exceptions) from a period between 2017 and 2018 while I was living alone, and religiously writing and experimenting everyday with new topics. I was surviving the anxiety and depression that accompanied the time and working through the recovery of my personal identity after the end of a particularly tumultuous romantic relationship gone sideways. I wasn't exactly healthy. At the worst of times, I was deeply paranoid, anxious and obsessive. There were even times I considered breathing a burden and waking life a nightmare.

At the best of times, I was laying down the groundwork to my current approach to life and setting the foundations to the career I'm continuing to help blossom and watching coalesce into the future. I was consistently writing poetry to post to my tumblr page, which would eventually become the manuscript to a recent collection of poetry that I released around the same time, *A Short Journey into the Land of the Dead*. Some poetry from this period gave root to the poetry I have been working into a manuscript today, that I hope to release into the wild soon. Needless to say, I was experiencing and feeling a lot of things at the time, and pushing myself to grow into the writer and person I've longed to become.

I did my best not to edit this book too much. All of the feelings in my writing, I kept in tact. Some of the grammar, I corrected, and a few of the phrases, I reworded for clarity's sake. I wanted to put my best work forward without destroying the integrity of the notes, but also without sacrificing any of my dignity in the process. Personal names, for instance, I've removed and left as blank spaces in the writing, a practice I picked up from poet Jorie Graham, but also meant to serve as a screen between details that I think are too personal to share and not necessary to display. My intention with this work isn't to air out my dirty laundry, but to highlight an emotional journey and to create play between the individual fragments of writing created at completely separate times, in various moods and with differing perspectives.

I never expected that I would find the return to these random bits of writing enjoyable, but it was a lot of fun digging through everything to choose a selection that I thought would be worthy of presenting to an audience.

Nothing written here was supposed to see the light of day. It was meant to remain a secret forever. If this book has taught me anything, it's to relax and recognize that I don't need to keep everything to myself, that in the small moments you think that no one is looking, you have the opportunity to be completely yourself. But it's okay if someone *is* looking. Little moments like this make our experience unique and interesting, and what could be more worthy of celebration than this? I welcome you to look and come celebrate with me this excursion into myself as an exercise in vulnerability, and also, hopefully, to enjoy knowing what goes on inside the mind of the weirdo that stands before you.

Nicholas Bonarski
April 26, 2023
Grand Rapids, MI

And to see the other side
to see things a mess
slipping backwards.

All The Things You Never Asked

I don't trust my heart's leap

as much as I trust time's parachute,
which allows me to leap several times more.

At what point do I bend

           far enough that light stays still

                  inside of me?

           I would never bend at all

        the echoes are what haunt the hallway,

not so much the mistakes, but how they were perceived,

the hum thereafter:

that echoes are not bodies,

but could it be true?

Could you read my poems the way a dog

greets a dog?

I'll tell you where I've been without saying at all.

I guess the truth is that no one is safe from the problems of art.

I shake my head.

The cool breeze

satisfies

the burning comet,

of course, I was triggered by that falling

in love thing.

I'm dumb,

taking defeat.

So small I might forget,
        you may forget me, too
            or in the coming hour forget me not.

      So soft, your soul, a ripple in the blanket
            or morning shaking the earth

the way the light pushes the water that presence forms:

a wave, and threadbare, we've abstained

        but no longer.

    I need to:
.Watch *From Up On Poppy Hill*
.
.

Hey nick

    M: hey, what going on? You okay?

N: no not really, I'm feeling bad.

    M: what about?

N: I'm so tired of talking about animals.

    M: then don't. Tell her you're cute animal'd out for

    the time being.

N: I think I will.

    Did I do something wrong?

watching the edge of the pool

disappear,

the water

                  falls away into nothingness

the face I saw so clear

for nearly each day

vanished

and with him brought the song

                       of dawn,

light which I folded into words,

a paper swan

 released into the pool's fragile wings

        parting behind him,

and his gaze gone,

not to be again

went away with the summer.

Lost in layers of touch,

               and its many prickles of hope,

                  a fist that closes, a fragile flower
                         two tragedies,
                         their violence

       and a will, each attempting the stone...

I just sink.

Lately I've been writing so much poetry and so many stories that I haven't really taken up stock in my own life. I feel like I'm neglecting myself or not being a real person, so I just want to say that I'm here and I'm real.

Yesterday was the first time I've cleaned in over a month. My home feels better to me now, like I'm not living at the bottom of a hole. My next step will be to take care of the old food in the refrigerator and then to get my trash situation together. I need to take the trash out by this Thursday— no *ifs, ands* or *buts!* And most importantly the kitty litter. They need to have clean litter and I'm sort of dropping the ball here. I need to start routinely cleaning their box. Other things I need to do: give myself a haircut. It's getting pretty messy and I want it to be short again. I might just get it done professionally this time. Also, I need to schedule some time for Rumi to get an appointment with the vet. She's a pretty active cat and very happy, but I can't just skip her check ups because she seems well. I need to make sure I know her health needs.

If there's anything else I need to do, it's to motivate myself to make an announcement about _____. People need to know it's out and I would like to explain why it's so late. If anything has bothered me the most, I think it's been the delays in producing it that killed my excitement and filled me with doubt about my writing.

I think it should be okay though. I think I know what to do now. I also need to make room for love. I've been feeling scared lately, especially now about everyone... my friends mostly. I feel lame. I wish we were connected again. I wish everything felt balanced and level again. I want to help my friends shine. I feel too in front of everyone.

I'm feeling sort of strange today.

Don't make me break my heart anymore,
you're more words than I know what to do with.

Story idea:

Cara is on a disappearing train. She's left home to find
her boyfriend, Mox, who disappeared from the face
of the earth one day after going to pay off a debt he
owed.

Sometimes, I think we have to have hearts of gold

because metallic and cold don't break as easily as flesh, red and warm.

No wonder we're all robots
with lock-box mechanisms.

We're in the middle of conversation
when, suddenly,
I realize
he's talking to himself

so, I start talking to myself
standing next to him when, suddenly,
he realizes
I'm talking to him.

So I start talking to him,

then,
we're in the middle of conversation
when, suddenly,
another guy
starts talking to him,

but he starts talking to himself
while the other guy talks
to him,
and I
start talking to myself

because who am I talking to?

And the other guy still thinks my friend's
talking to me,

> when the other guy realizes
> he's talking to himself,
> even though he's
> talking to me
> and thinks,
> *I'm* really *talking to him.*

So he starts talking to himself,

> and I start talking to myself,
> but my friend,
> he's talking
> to both of us now
> while we talk to ourselves.

But once he starts talking
to himself, *again,*
the other guy says:
"Hey, he's talking to me about me."
And I think,

> *Damn, buddy, aren't we all.*

Sometimes _____
talks to himself while I'm standing
next to him.

Imagine his surprise
when I don't respond.

The green bean believes she's pregnant.
We wait in a small church,
                    countryside waning

                    immaculate Christ,
                    immaculate pea.

She touches my arm,
her navel: A pod full of pearls,
                    beads above the cross

                    slide one by one
                    underneath her fingers,

rosewood between knuckles (bead after bead after bead
                    after bead after bead).

N: man I feel bad now, like I'm a hateful person.

M: why? Because someone said "super" about your poem?
So you mean you're angry?

N: yeah..

now what?

It's all waiting underneath.
All there, waiting for you,

underneath

in the secret subways of mind,
missing luggage, wayward violinist,
 the kid with shades

waiting.
All of it.
The tags, the bells
the whistles,

it's where you want it
when you go to grab it.
You just have to
reach out
and—

Gone adrift, too far out of this world.

When am I coming down? I've flown so far

without fuel,

I just spin in the dark with the slate sky alight,

marking my days of waste.

Open, close, ok.

What do I need?

you probably need to _____.

One petal will do,
from your favorite flower.

M: you okay?

N:yeah.

M: what is it?

N: I just wish it felt good to do the right thing.

M: you don't think you did the right thing though.

N: I think I did, I just didn't do it the right way.

M: what do you mean? How so?

N: I'm not sure what way would have been better, but I wish I had been more personal about it.

I don't want the arms of angels
to enfold me.
I perceive a strange calamity
                dripping from a sparrow's wing,

                    the misty perfume of skunk
trailing in

ahead of the dog.

Disengage the engine,

we don't need much to orbit.

There's only 20 seconds left until the first,

until the second.

                              The world doesn't move without,

                    it moves within, willing
                              flowing

out of the mist
and into.

Searching for you on the wall will be difficult,

you will be among the millions.

We'll be lovers, I'm certain. We will have known each

other from a time before,
we just haven't discovered each other yet.

Like lithium ion batteries.

Become so small,

the tiniest

grain of sand in a statue.

It was like everyone knew without knowing. And they worked to get things to where they needed to be. I watched it all, this mechanism correcting itself without me. My being the little cog that didn't serve a purpose, I stopped turning. Yet, I was as much a part of it, watching them turn, my place a silent one. I wanted to do as much as I could, though, I could only do nothing. If I could only be more than this, I think I'd like that.

Shift within the structure.

N:something feels incredibly wrong.

    M:what do you think it is?

N:I'm not sure.

    M: what do you think it is?

N:everything is really echoey in here.

    M:where are you, man?

N: I'm in an empty room.

    M: you're in an empty room?

    M: are you there?

N: yes.

    M: you're in another place?

N: yes.

    M: you shouldn't show this to anyone.

N:you're right.

    M: you're alone.

B: yes.

    M: but wait, you're not you?

B: you're right.

    M: but what are you doing here in this empty room?

B: I'm not sure... is there something I should be doing?

    M: whatever you want to do.

B: whatever I want to do.

    M: hey, man.

growing beard and a pair of glasses
colored pencils and sand
arching comet in the sky above
open mouthed, a polished pearl

The inside of the house

may not be a reflection

of the outside,

nor the outside

in.

I was taking care of everything in a haunted mansion. I knew nothing would harm me, but a tiger growled and it freaked me out and woke me up.

When your dreams coalesce to form an answer you've been seeking and the voices in your head chant collectively "Do it!" without prompt.

So we were playing this game and it's about combining two words as "clues" to something sweet happening.

Don't let the moment unzip... hold it back— at arm's length.

I was so paranoid.

    N:I'm not sure what I should do.

(the moment leaves)

Part of my problem with this writing is I haven't been staying *present*. I've been trying to control *too much* of it. I should let it be what it wants to be, not force it to conform to my *vision* of what it *could be*. I should regard it as having its own life.

I'm an

antithetical waste burning in a heap of garbage,

flames bending the corners of
a page that no one, not even the sky wants to read.

Wow, great, well hats off to ~~you~~ me.

M:nick you sound exhausted to be totally honest. You need
to relax and sleep. I know there are a few things that need to
be done, but seriously, man, you need to catch up with *you*.
The book's coming, and the writing is on its way.

Eye contact is weird. I startle too many people, and myself.

Dear self esteem issues and path of destruction,

I'm sorry. For whatever reason, I've fallen back into you, and I'm sorry because I don't want to be held by you anymore. I'm moving on. I'm worth more. I'm not a bad person, and I have the capability of moving forward. I'm abandoning plans and living in the moment where love is. I know my situation is unique. My condition is my own, and I can escape you. So I'm leaving.

Goodbye.

I was up in the tower of some mansion, and we were going to be attacked by a mob of people. Some of us had to stay, but I had to climb down and out of it for some reason.

_____ was there by the window. She was going to use a rope to do something. I've seen this mansion before. It's a place I recognized as "work" once when I worked for the schools.

I climb out of the window into the snow and see two kids eying the ladder I was going to use to climb down. They saw me and my presence scared them off. They were little kids, after all, and they wouldn't have known what they were doing anyway.

This ladder was an old iron bar ladder. Black iron, and as I climb down, I realize the house is full of parlors. An odd observation. I can see them through the windows as I pass by. They all remind me of rooms from a gimmicky haunted house attraction, one that I knew as a kid when I lived near Greenville. I have a vague memory of it, but it's been too long.

On the edge of the house, climbing down this ladder, I start eating a little bit of ice cream from a plastic cup (lol whatever helps, I guess) using a broken piece of glass as my spoon. Snow is falling outside and the iron rungs of the ladder are freezing. But I have to climb down the ladder regardless.

I don't finish the ice cream because eventually the shard of glass breaks in my mouth. That's when I spit it out and reach the bottom.

No longer stuck on the ladder, I climb back it onto it, barefoot as Aomame (I guess I've entered *1Q84* by Haruki Murakami)... and climb down again, stopping to feel the breeze.

Finally on the other side, I'm ushered into an old looking hotel that's really my grandparent's house. It's interesting. There are two tunnels that split off of the main entrance, like you would see in an aquarium, only they're outside. And green. Where they split off, one goes in a square to the left, and the other in a square to the right.

A person is waiting at the entrance in a brown leather duster, ready to take the ticket from my hand. I have a ticket in my hand, I notice. I feel like I'm being rude. They were hanging out in the tunnel playing a game and talking and I obviously wasn't supposed to be there. But they take the ticket and point me in the right direction.

Down the hall and to your left. I follow the path and there I see my grandma in this busy dining restaurant, sun cascading in through the many windows at the back of the building. The carpet is red, the room supported by white pillars and a few steps lead down a level to the dining room floor. I see my brother and he's chatting it up with someone. They just sat down to a strange sort of tart breakfast.

Later on, I'm at _____'s house. I've seen a place like theirs before, like _____'s old house, actually. Just like it. _____ sends me upstairs for something and _____ sees me. He comes out of his room, stops and scowls. I think I forgot to return something to him, and immediately thought of a book I never actually borrowed from him. I go into _____'s room, and look inside the closet for something. I have to change my clothes and go somewhere. The details are hazy. But I wake up with the impression that _____ was mad at me for being there.

Hi nick! you are finally caught back up.

Spitting broken glass,
cracked, used as a spoon.

Careful not to spit the shards
where I plan to walk.

What's on your mind?

M: mmm more sleep.

In my dream there is this square chinned man with straight, orange hair down to his lower back. I'm not sure why we're hanging out, but we're at my old house. And _____ was there, the guy that used to live in my apartment before me, but he is in the room with the glass doors making cheese sticks. And I just go and eat one without permission! Rude! But I totally didn't leave one, I just took it and he comes back and I offer to repay him. But that's not right. You shouldn't just eat another person's cheese stick and say "oh, sorry, about that." You just have to leave them alone.

And then there's this concert I'm at with _____ and I tell him I don't like the musical artist we're there to see. I've heard his stuff before and think he's like a crap knock off of Conor Oberst. But _____ says it's about how the artist is doing it that he likes.

"What you say when the puzzle is complete without using your words."

I saw a crow perched on something in my dream. A bird feeder? A branch? I'm pretty aware of it being the symbol of my destiny.

5179

I might be crazy,

I might be a "stable genius."

I feel stupid.

It may be easier to believe myself a chest.

I think I'm boring myself to death.

I'm just a little kid.

How many more nails can we drive into this coffin?

Life is made out of mistakes
and the others we make to recover from them.

Or am I just trying to avoid the ugly truth?

My head isn't thinking very well today. I'm down on my
mind. Do I need anything?

The pain stopped the second I really admitted I was jealous.

Am I messed up?

No you're fine.

I'm fine... I'm scared.

No need, little one. I'm here.

I'm sorry.

All the things you never asked,

I just figured that you didn't want to know.

There in the river
the question began with "Where"
but never resolved.

"What do you think it means?" _____ has never asked such a thing before. But if I had told them it wouldn't have mattered. It would have slipped through their fingers as sure as ginger. As sure as it did through mine. I suppose it wasn't so bad, leaving it carved into the cement, the last glyph. I had done exactly what I intended... both a blessing and a curse.

The woman who appeared in my dream was so angelic, so quiet. She sat alone looking out the window of the guest bedroom, far from everything and everyone. She wouldn't look at me, but she didn't look, not because she was hurt, or bored, or dissuaded. She genuinely didn't see me. Looking with some degree of detachment toward the sky, maybe at the moon, she kept on looking out the window. I wanted to stay with her. To be by her side more than anyone. I still do. I have this feeling, really deep down, that she's a part of me; the part I said I need to separate from. I'm of the belief that I can't and shouldn't, yet will need to in some sense. She's a very sweet part of my life. She is my _____ I feel like, in a way. But it seems like her choice, not mine.

Stress bears down on the beams. The bridge is in a state of delicate composure. It spans the North Atlantic Ocean, adjoining two bodies of land separated by the desperately cold, far reaching waters that toss and turn below it.

A fascinating achievement to have created something so terrifyingly large as to stretch across the entire North Atlantic Ocean. To craft such an unimaginable piece of architecture comes at an enormous cost. Many lives were lost in its construction. But to be frank, one life is too many to lose over something as frightening as this vast highway, cutting through ice, currents, and waves.

"We never wanted to die."
"Not for something like this..."
"Couldn't we have settled for planes and ships?"

Nearly a month away from completion one of several tragedies occurred. Two workers strung from the underbelly of the bridge, wiring lights and communication lines, were swept away by a powerful gust of wind and dropped hundreds of feet into the freezing drifts of ice and water. Their bodies were never recovered, though, a placard was placed in their honor. Still, the work kept on going.

Reach! Tantalus cries
and the people reach their hands
to catch the nectar.

I'm really hurting. It's like I've stopped caring about everything. I've stopped caring about living. My whole mind is against me. My body is just shutting down. I was so hurt, I stopped enjoying Battlestar Galactica... I hurt like it's impossible to do anything or live at all. Like life is absolutely meaningless.

It's like my heart just won't sit still.
>Everything wants to fly away.

I hear my mother calling my name
and the mutters of a friend.

>They aren't quite the same, ringing,

the engine.

>One fades,

>gasps and flashes,

>sputters , gasps again,

>gone.

outside
the wailing sound

Cold rain, Warsaw.
Ornamentation
and workflow,
what we know
will converge:
a traffic jam of
words,
regular words
worth water
and bread,
brush strokes
of bromide,
Bruises.

Birds of paradise

papery and personal

perfectly purposed.

Turning a large key,

one thousand loose pages fall out
heavy with spilled ink.

All that I could do was sleep.

I had a dream about _____, and we were both at a party. He asks me if I hate him, and I tell him no, actually, I really like you a lot. We end up going on a walk through an old building together and it's cool being friends with him. I hold him in pretty high esteem in my mind.

We could wait here with words or return to waking.

m:hey nick, what's up?

N: I'm just really sad. I'm missing things around me, and I think I've grown egotistical, inconsiderate, and critical.

Am I not in control of my own life?

How can I forgive myself what I don't regret?

Thank you for being so amazing all of the time. I really appreciate you and enjoy you and love being around you a lot. You're really great and I'm over the moon about you.

I had a great dream last night about hanging out with
_____ and walking to a piece of construction
equipment that we were taking to a worksite nearby. At
some point, I also walked around with _____ and she
would bring up _____ but it was like she didn't know
that anything happened between us. I remember being
somewhere near _____ park and wanting to go there to
meet with someone else. But I'm not sure where else I was
headed...

So we go as far as we can, and appreciate the little things.

To properly close the door
    (as a door is made to shut
   and open, maybe, to another
     hand, a new face)

Use bravery that, in the hinges
      resides.

Check that it's working properly, that the
    handles won't fall off
as it's necessary sometimes to tighten them

And before you leave
    check that it's locked—

yes, it is locked, and the furniture's gone—

yes, the furniture is gone and

the room and the keys are yours.

www.ingramcontent.com/pod-product-compliance
Lightning Source LLC
Chambersburg PA
CBHW060346130626
46553CB00003B/1107